my **revisi⏻n** notes

D0314077

AQA GCSE
Computer
Science
Computing
Fundamentals

my **revisi⏻n** notes

AQA GCSE
Computer Science
Computing Fundamentals

Steve Cushing

The publishers would like to thank the following for permission to reproduce copyright material:

Photo credits:

24 *tl* © Jakub Semeniuk/iStockphoto, *tr* © Konstantin Shevtsov – Fotolia, *cl* © Yordan Marinov – Fotolia, *cr* © Tatiana Popova/iStockphoto, *bl* © Alysta – Fotolia, *br* © Siede Preis/Photodisc/Getty Images; **25** *tl* © yuka26 – Fotolia, *tr* © Sweetym/iStockphoto, *bl* © Mike McCune/iStockphoto, *br* © Konstantin Shevtsov – Fotolia; **27** © Godfried Edelman/iStockphoto; **29** © Robert Gray/Gray Publishing; **32** © Robert Gray/Gray Publishing; **66** *tl* © masterpiece – Fotolia, *tr* © pizuttipics – Fotolia, *bl* © Mark Evans/iStockphoto, *br* © bloomua - Fotolia

Every effort has been made to trace all copyright holders, but if any have been inadvertently overlooked the Publishers will be pleased to make the necessary arrangements at the first opportunity.

Although every effort has been made to ensure that website addresses are correct at time of going to press, Hodder Education cannot be held responsible for the content of any website mentioned. It is sometimes possible to find a relocated web page by typing in the address of the home page for a website in the URL window of your browser.

Hachette UK's policy is to use papers that are natural, renewable and recyclable products and made from wood grown in sustainable forests. The logging and manufacturing processes are expected to conform to the environmental regulations of the country of origin.

Orders: please contact Bookpoint Ltd, 130 Milton Park, Abingdon, Oxon OX14 4SB. Telephone: (44) 01235 827720. Fax: (44) 01235 400454. Lines are open 9.00–17.00, Monday to Saturday, with a 24-hour message answering service. Visit our website at www.hoddereducation.co.uk

© Steve Cushing 2013

First published in 2013 by

Hodder Education

An Hachette UK Company,

London NW1 3BH

Impression number 5 4 3 2 1

Year 2017 2016 2015 2014 2013

Cover photo © Aleksandr Bedrin – Fotolia

Typeset by Datapage (India) Pvt. Ltd.

Printed in Spain

A catalogue record for this title is available from the British Library

ISBN 978 1 444 193862

Get the most from this book

This book will help you revise for the AQA GCSE Computer Science Computing Fundamentals exam. You can use the contents list on page 7 to plan your revision, topic by topic. Tick each box when you have:

1 revised and understood a topic

2 tested yourself

3 checked your answers.

You can also keep track of your revision by ticking off each topic heading through the book. You may find it helpful to add your own notes as you work through each topic.

Tick to track your progress

Exam tips

Throughout the book there are Exam tips that explain how you can boost your final grade.

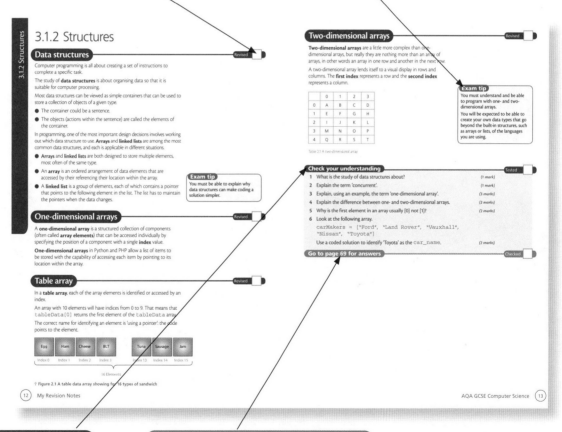

Check your understanding

Use these questions at the end of each section to make sure that you have understood every topic.

Go to page 69 for answers

Check your answers at the back of the book.

Contents and revision planner

3.1.1 Constants, variables and data types

Data and information

A common mistake is to confuse the terms **data** and **information**; there are distinct differences between these concepts:

- **Data** can consist of facts or statistics out of context and used for analysis. It can be numbers, characters, symbols or images that are processed by a computer.

- **Information** can be a sentence of words, a sequence of numbers or a series of images that have been put into a **context**, which is what gives the data meaning.

In order to change data into information, it needs to become part of a structure. For example, 'NN' and the number 12 are **data** but when we know they are part of a postcode, 'NN12', they become **information** as they have meaning.

The difference between a constant and a variable

In mathematics, a variable is a symbol or letter, such as x or y, that represents a value. Variables are used in computer programming to store specific values within a program. They are assigned both a data type and a value.

Some values are stored permanently: the data is **constant**. Other things are always changing: the data is **variable**.

Throughout computer programming:

- **variables** are data entities whose values can be altered

- **constants** are data entities whose values cannot be altered.

Most programming languages use **variables** and **constants** to store different **types** of data.

Naming variables

- The name of a variable can be as short as a single letter but not a single number.

- The name of a variable can start with a letter or an underscore '_'.

- After the first character of the variable, the name of the variable can include letters, numbers, or underscores in any combination.

- The name of a variable cannot be one of the words that the programming language has reserved for its own use.

In most programming languages, you cannot tell the difference between a variable and a constant by their name – the difference is in how they are used.

> **Exam tip**
>
> You will need to understand when to use constants and variables in problem-solving scenarios and how to name them.

The purpose of data types within code

Data can be stored in many different forms, known as **data types**.

A computer uses special internal codes to keep track of the different types of data it processes.

Most programming languages require the programmer to declare the data type of every data object.

It is the data type that determines the actions (for instance, searching, sorting or calculating) that can be performed on the data when it is held within a program or field of a database or a spreadsheet.

The most common data types you will have used are called **primitive data types**.

Primitive data types are predefined types of data which are supported by the programming language.

Data types

Integer

An **integer** data type deals with whole numbers (not decimal numbers, which use a different data type):

a member of the set of positive whole numbers (1, 2, 3, . . .), negative whole numbers (–1, –2, –3, . . .), and zero (0)

a complete unit or entity.

Real

A **real** data type contains numeric data in a decimal form.

It is used in situations where more accurate information is required than an integer can provide as an integer is a whole number.

Date/Time

The **date/time** data type is used to store dates and times.

Dates and times can appear in many different formats. Some countries have different methods of representing the date:

11/06/2012 means 6 November 2012 in the USA.

11/06/2012 means 11 June 2012 in the UK.

Floating-point numbers

The following are floating-point numbers:

4.0   –133.8

Computers are integer machines and are capable of representing real numbers by using codes.

The most popular code for representing real numbers is called the IEEE Floating-Point Standard.

Floating-point numbers have no fixed number of digits before and after the decimal point – the decimal point can float.

The number of digits before and after the decimal point is sometimes set, this is called fixed-point representations.

Most floating-point numbers that a computer can represent are just approximations.

> **Exam tip**
>
> You are expected to use data types appropriate to a programming task.
>
> As a minimum, you must know about integer, Boolean, real, character and string data types and how they are represented in the programming languages you are using.

Computers are often slow when processing floating-point numbers.

Because mathematics with floating-point numbers requires a great deal of computing power, many microprocessors come with a chip, called a floating-point unit (FPU), designed to performing floating-point arithmetic.

FPUs are sometimes called maths coprocessors or numeric coprocessors.

Floating-point numbers are less accurate than fixed-point numbers. A challenge in programming with floating-point numbers is to ensure that the approximations lead to reasonable results.

Floating-point numbers are used because computers can handle a very large range of them.

String

As well as integers and floating point numbers, programmers need to represent text in a program. Text, referred to as a 'string', is composed of a set of characters that can also contain spaces and numbers. For example, the word 'hamburger' and the phrase 'He has eaten 5 hamburgers' are both strings.

Boolean

The **Boolean** data type represents the values of true/false or yes/no.

The primitive data type of a Boolean is **logical**.

Boolean logic is a type of mathematical comparison. It is used to evaluate true or false.

Boolean operator	What it means
AND	True if and only if both sides are true
OR	True if either side is true (or both are true)
NOT	Changes true to false and false to true

Boolean logic evaluates every expression to either **true** or **false**. Therefore, substituting true or false for each of these expressions outputs the same value:

```
if (true) AND (true) then print "rain"
if (true AND true) then print "rain"
```

If either statement after the 'if' was not true, nothing would be printed.

There are six arithmetic tests that can be used to create Boolean values, as follows:

Operator	Name of operator
<	Less than
<=	Less than or equal to
==	Equal to
!=	Not equal to
>=	Greater than or equal to
>	Greater than

All the operators within the table above have obvious meanings and can be used together with Boolean operators within conditional statements.

> **Exam tip**
> You must understand and be able to program using Boolean operators.

1 In mathematics which of the following are integers:

  8 5 103 −1.33 1¾ 98 3.14 1500.45 −935 *(7 marks)*

2 What is a real data type? *(2 marks)*

3 Give **two** reasons why a programmer would wish to use an integer data type rather than a real data type. *(2 marks)*

4 Consider the following sentence and write it as a Boolean: *(4 marks)*

  When the door is open and it is cold outside I have to wear my coat.

5 In programming what is a 'string'? *(4 marks)*

6 What is a 'variable' in programming? *(1 mark)*

7 What does the following code do? *(3 marks)*

```
If (($wet && $cold) || ($poor && $hungry)) {
                    Print "I'm sad!";
                        }
```

8 The primary purpose of software is to turn data into: *(1 mark)*

  a) a web site

  b) information

  c) programs

  d) an object.

Go to page 69 for answers Checked

3.1.2 Structures

Data structures

Revised

Computer programming is all about creating a set of instructions to complete a specific task.

The study of **data structures** is about organising data so that it is suitable for computer processing.

Most data structures can be viewed as simple containers that can be used to store a collection of objects of a given type.

- The container could be a sentence.
- The objects (actions within the sentence) are called the elements of the container.

In programming, one of the most important design decisions involves working out which data structure to use. **Arrays** and **linked lists** are among the most common data structures, and each is applicable in different situations.

- **Arrays** and **linked lists** are both designed to store multiple elements, most often of the same type.
- An **array** is an ordered arrangement of data elements that are accessed by their referencing their location within the array.
- A **linked list** is a group of elements, each of which contains a pointer that points to the following element in the list. The list has to maintain the pointers when the data changes.

> **Exam tip**
>
> You must be able to explain why data structures can make coding a solution simpler.

One-dimensional arrays

Revised

A **one-dimensional array** is a structured collection of components (often called **array elements**) that can be accessed individually by specifying the position of a component with a single **index** value.

One-dimensional arrays in Python and PHP allow a list of items to be stored with the capability of accessing each item by pointing to its location within the array.

Table array

Revised

In a **table array**, each of the array elements is identified or accessed by an index.

An array with 10 elements will have indices from 0 to 9. That means that `tableData[0]` returns the first element of the `tableData` array.

The correct name for identifying an element is 'using a pointer': the code points to the element.

↑ **Figure 2.1 A table data array showing for 16 types of sandwich**

My Revision Notes

Two-dimensional arrays

Revised

Two-dimensional arrays are a little more complex than one-dimensional arrays, but really they are nothing more than an array of arrays, in other words an array in one row and another in the next row.

A two-dimensional array lends itself to a visual display in rows and columns. The **first index** represents a row and the **second index** represents a column.

	0	1	2	3
0	A	B	C	D
1	E	F	G	H
2	I	J	K	L
3	M	N	O	P
4	Q	R	S	T

Table 2.1 A two-dimensional array

> **Exam tip**
>
> You must understand and be able to program with one- and two-dimensional arrays.
>
> You will be expected to be able to create your own data types that go beyond the built-in structures, such as arrays or lists, of the languages you are using.

Check your understanding

Tested

1 What is the study of data structures about? *(1 mark)*

2 Explain the term 'concurrent'. *(1 mark)*

3 Explain, using an example, the term 'one-dimensional array'. *(3 marks)*

4 Explain the difference between one- and two-dimensional arrays. *(2 marks)*

5 Why is the first element in an array usually [0] not [1]? *(2 marks)*

6 Look at the following array.

```
carMakers = ["Ford", "Land Rover", "Vauxhall",
"Nissan", "Toyota"]
```

Use a coded solution to identify 'Toyota' as the car_name. *(2 marks)*

Go to page 69 for answers

Checked

3.1.3 Program flow control

To program correctly you will need to consider program design (planning) and the actual program coding.

The name given to planning is called **control structured programming**.

There are three fundamental control structures:

● A **sequence** is a set of instructions or actions in order, meaning that each action follows the previous action (see Figure 3.1)

● A **selection** control structure involves a choice (**if–then–else**).

● A **looping** (**iteration**) control structure involves repeating actions.

↑ **Figure 3.1 A simple sequence of actions**

Exam tip

You must be able to use the different flow control blocks (i.e. sequencing, selection and iteration) to solve a problem.

You must be able to show your understanding of structure when you are designing coded solutions to problems.

Defining flow of control

Revised

Program flow control, or flow of control, can be defined as the order in which a program is executed or evaluated.

There are three different flow control structures that every programming language supports; however, different programming languages may support different kinds of control flow statements.

Exam tip

You need to understand how problems can be broken down into smaller problems and how these steps can be represented by the use of devices such as flowcharts and structure diagrams.

The flowchart symbols denoting the basic building blocks of structural programming are shown in Figure 3.2.

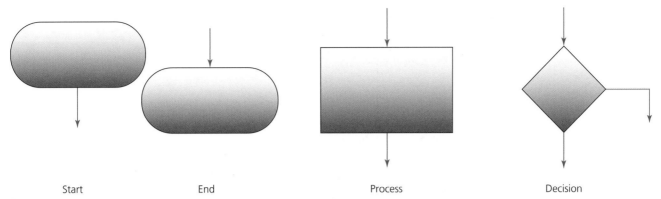

Start   End   Process   Decision

↑ **Figure 3.2 Flowchart symbols for start, end, process and decision**

The **Start** symbol represents the start of a process:

  It has exactly one output.

The **End** symbol represents the end of a process:

  It has exactly one input.

  It generally contains either 'End' or 'Return' depending on its function in the overall process of the flowchart.

A **Process** symbol represents some operation that is carried out on an element of data:

  It has exactly one input and one output.

  It contains a brief description describing the process being carried out on the data.

A **Decision** symbol represents a Boolean choice:

  It has exactly one input and two outputs.

  It should contain a question that clearly has only two possible answers.

  The two outputs are labelled with the two answers to the question in order to show the direction of the logic flow depending upon the decision made.

> **Exam tip**
>
> You must understand and be able to describe the basic building blocks of coded solutions (i.e. sequencing, selection and iteration).

Looping/Iteration   Revised ☐

Iteration is where a statement is executed in a loop until the program reaches a certain state or the intended operations have been applied to every data element of an array.

If you look at Figure 3.3, you can see that the iteration/loop keeps on occurring until a false statement is reached.

  While statements are efficient loops that will continue to loop until the condition is false.

  Do–While statements are also efficient loops that will continue to loop until the condition is false. They are identical to **While** statements except that they start with **Do** and the **While** condition comes after the braces.

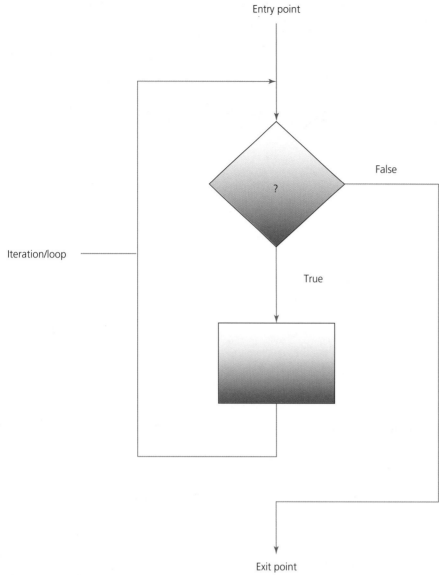

Entry point

?

False

True

Iteration/loop

Exit point

⬆ **Figure 3.3 A flowchart showing an iteration/loop**

1 Explain with simple examples the basic building blocks of coded solutions. *(3 marks)*

2 Represent the following code as a simple flowchart. *(4 marks)*

```
if condition is true
then
    perform instructions in Block1
else
    perform instructions in Block2
endif
```

3 Design a simple flowchart to show the actions of a single move in a snakes and ladders game. *(6 marks)*

Go to page 70 for answers ●━━━━━━━━━━━━━━━━━━━━━━━ Checked

3.1.4 Procedures and functions

Defining procedures and functions
Revised

Procedures and **functions** feature in all programming languages. They are named blocks of code (**subroutines**) that can be used and re-used to perform specific tasks.

Their purpose is to allow the repetition of certain sections of a program or calculation many times.

They also assist in the modulation of code by allowing themselves to be called from any point within a program solution.

> A **procedure** is a block of code that performs a task without returning a value.

> A **function** is very similar to a procedure except that it returns a value.

There are two types of function:

> **User-defined functions** are created by the user for a program.

> **Built-in functions** are part of the programming language.

> **Exam tip**
>
> You must be able to explain what procedures and functions are in programming terms.
>
> You must be able to explain when the use of a procedure or function would make sense and would simplify the coded solution.
>
> You must be able to write and use simple procedures and functions.

Built-in functions
Revised

Built-in functions are also called 'library functions':

> They are provided by the **system**.

> They are stored in **library files**.

The real power of any programming language comes from the built-in functions.

> Built-in functions are always available for your program to call.

> Built-in functions are very useful and save a lot of effort in writing code to perform common tasks.

> **Exam tip**
>
> You need to be able to describe common built-in functions in your chosen languages.

Parameters
Revised

Procedures and functions would have limited use if it wasn't for a feature called **parameters**. In computer programming, a **parameter** is a special kind of variable.

It is used in a subroutine to refer to one of the pieces of data provided as input to the subroutine. It therefore allows the passing of values to the procedure or function for use inside it.

> **Exam tip**
>
> You should be able to explain what a parameter is and how to use parameters when creating efficient solutions to problems.

Check your understanding

1 What is the purpose of procedures and functions in programming
   languages?
   (2 marks)

2 What is the main difference between a procedure and a function?
   (2 marks)

Go to page 71 for answers

Checked

3.1.5 Scope of variables, constants, functions and procedures

● **Procedure scope** refers to when a variable can be read and modified only from within the procedure in which it is declared.

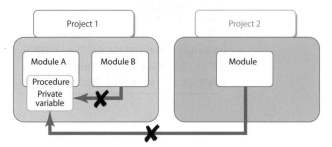

↑ **Figure 5.1 Procedure scope**

● **Module scope** refers to when a variable is declared before and outside of any procedure within a regular program module.

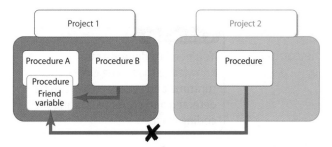

↑ **Figure 5.2 Module scope**

● **Project scope** is declared using the **public** command keyword. Variables with project scope can be read and modified from any procedure contained within any module within the program or project.

● **Global scope** variables have the capability of being accessed from anywhere within the project that contains their declaration as well as from other projects that refer to that initial project.

Exam tip

You must be able to identify what value a particular variable will hold at a given point in the code.

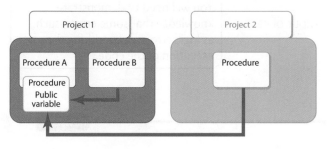

↑ **Figure 5.3 Global scope**

Check your understanding
Tested ☐

1 What is global scope? *(2 marks)*

2 In terms of scope, briefly describe what is meant by: *(2 marks)*

   a) local variable

   b) global variable.

Go to page 71 for answers
Checked ☐

3.1.6 Error handling

Types of error

There are basically three types of error that computer programmers encounter when writing software. These are:

- syntax errors
- run-time errors
- logic errors.

Syntax errors

Syntax errors or, as they are sometimes known, **format errors** occur when the programmer fails to obey one of the grammar rules of the programming language that they are using.

Typically, this maybe down to using the wrong case, placing punctuation in positions where it should not exist or failing to insert punctuation where it should be placed within the code.

Run-time errors

Run-time errors occur whenever the program instructs the computer to carry out an operation that it is either not designed to do or slow to do.

Logic errors

Logic errors are typically the most difficult kind of errors to detect and rectify. This is usually down to the fact that there is no obvious indication of the error within the software.

The program runs successfully; however, it does not behave in the manner it was designed to. In other words, it will produce incorrect results.

The most common reasons for logic errors are usually a consequence of one of the following:

- The programmer did not understand the manner in which the program was meant to behave.
- The programmer did not understand the individual behaviour of each operation that was part of the program.
- The programmer was careless.

> **Exam tip**
> You need to be able to discuss and identify the different types of error that can occur within code (i.e. syntax, run-time and logical).

> **Exam tip**
> You need to demonstrate knowledge that some errors, such as run-time and syntax errors, can be detected and corrected during the coding stage.

> **Exam tip**
> You will need to demonstrate knowledge that some errors, such as logic errors, occur during the execution of the code.

Testing code for errors

Dry-run testing

Dry-run testing is usually carried out on the **algorithm** which is written in pseudo-code or as part of a flowchart.

This form of testing is usually done prior to the program code being written. The main advantage of dry-run testing is that it enables programmers to spot errors even before they start writing code.

Testing for errors during the execution of code

The process of testing a program for errors during its execution is a cyclic activity called **debugging**.

To debug code effectively, two things are needed:

● the ability to **test each of the instructions** provided by a program
● the capability to **retrieve the information** about:
    ● the results of the instructions
    ● any changes in the program when the tests were carried out
    ● the error conditions
    ● what the program was doing when the error occurred.

Trace tables

A **trace table** is used to test algorithms to see if any logic errors occur while the algorithm is being processed.

Within the table, each column contains a variable and each row displays a numerical input to the algorithm and the resultant values of the variables.

step	now	last	count
1			
2			
3			

Table 6.1 A trace table

Exam tip

You need to demonstrate knowledge of how to detect errors at execution time and how to handle those errors to prevent the program from crashing.

Exam tip

You need to demonstrate knowledge of how to use trace tables to check your own code for errors.

You must understand that computer programs can be developed with tools to help the programmer detect and deal with errors.

Check your understanding

Tested

1   What are the three types of error that computer programmers encounter when writing software? *(3 marks)*

2   What is meant by a 'format error' and what is its correct name? *(4 marks)*

3   State what happens when programming statements are written in the wrong order and state the name for this type of error. *(3 marks)*

4   Which type of programming error is the hardest to detect and why? *(3 marks)*

5   What is the name given to the testing of software at the planning and flowchart stage? *(2 marks)*

6   What is a 'trace table'? *(2 marks)*

7   What is correcting errors in a program called? *(1 mark)*

   a) compiling

   b) debugging

   c) grinding

   d) interpreting.

Go to page 71 for answers

Checked

3.1.7 Handling external data

External data

It is not possible to hold all the data we need inside the program using arrays.

Sometimes the data has to be held externally, outside the program itself.

One example of this could be a dictionary. There would be far too much data in a dictionary to be held in an array.

All programs have to deal with **external data**.

All programs either accept **input** data from sources outside the coding of the program or produce some kind of **output**. Often they do both.

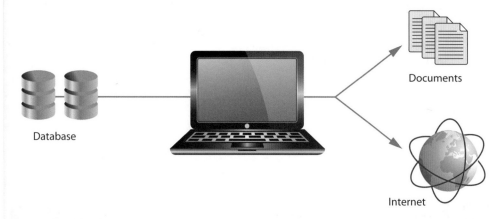

⬆ **Figure 7.1 Data held in an external database can be collected, analysed and passed on**

Reading and writing a text file ────────────── Revised ☐

Text files are a popular and convenient format that allows programs, created in a range of different languages, to handle external data.

When you write information to a text file, you are adding data to that file.

> **Exam tip**
> You need to demonstrate knowledge of how to use an external text file to read and write data in a way that is appropriate for the programming languages you choose to use and the problem being solved.

Reading and writing a database ────────────── Revised ☐

Reading and writing from a text document and holding data in a data string works fine for a large number of applications, but it cannot be used to store and retrieve large amounts of data. In such instances your program has to talk to a **database**.

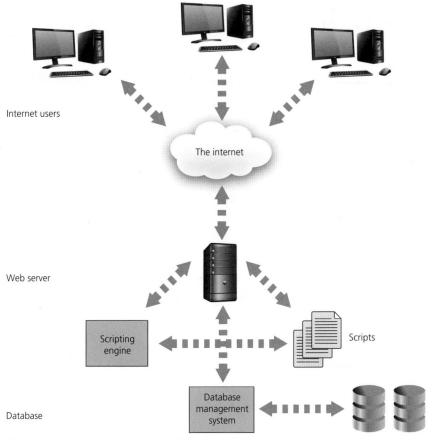

Internet users

The internet

Web server

Scripting engine

Scripts

Database management system

Database

↑ **Figure 7.2 Users access the website from the web server and the scripting engine accesses the database using SQL**

SQL (**Structured Query Language**) is used to communicate with a database.

Some of the common relational database management systems that use SQL are: Oracle, Sybase, Microsoft SQL Server, Microsoft Access and Ingres.

Standard SQL commands (see section 3.1.15.1) such as SELECT, INSERT, UPDATE, DELETE, CREATE and DROP can be used to accomplish almost everything that a programmer needs to do with a database.

> **Exam tip**
>
> You must be able to read and write data from an external database in a way that is appropriate for the programming languages used and the problem being solved.

Check your understanding
Tested

1. Using code, create a text file containing the names 'Steve Cushing' and 'Ian Cushing'.

(8 marks)

2. When would a programmer want to use a database to hold external data rather than a text document?

(2 marks)

3. List the **four** most common SQL commands.

(5 marks)

4. What is the SQL command to delete a column from an existing table?

(1 mark)

   a) Alter table

   b) Drop table

   c) Delete table

   d) Delete column

Go to page 72 for answers
Checked

3.1.8 Computer structure

3.1.8.1 Systems

Definition of a computer system

In its very basic form, a computer system can be looked at as nothing more than an **input**, a **process**, some **storage** and an **output**.

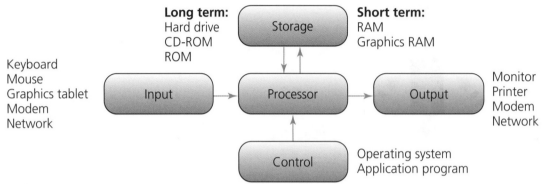

Long term:
Hard drive
CD-ROM
ROM

Storage

Short term:
RAM
Graphics RAM

Keyboard
Mouse
Graphics tablet
Modem
Network

Input → Processor → Output

Monitor
Printer
Modem
Network

Control

Operating system
Application program

↑ Figure 8.1 The definition of a computer system

The **input** of a computer system is usually provided by hardware devices in the form of digital data or commands. These devices could be:

● a keyboard

● a mouse

● a scanner

● a microphone.

↑ Figure 8.2 Input devices

The **processing** is carried out by a range of **hardware** (such as the processor on the motherboard, a graphics card or a soundcard) and **software** (such as the applications, utility programs and the operating system).

Hardware devices also provide the **output** from a computer system which is where the processed information is presented to the user in a readable and useable form. These devices could be:

● a monitor
● speakers
● a printer.

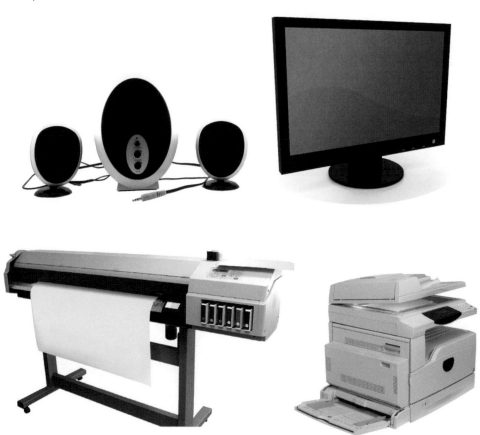

↑ **Figure 8.3 Output devices**

The importance of computer systems to the modern world

As time goes on, computer systems will become even more integral to our everyday lives.

Computer **chips** control many of the products we use each day.

We have come to depend on computer systems a great deal, taking advantage of the services that they offer and the data that they can store.

Reliability in computer systems is vitally important.

The consequences of failure

Malfunctions of computer systems can be catastrophic – both for organisations and for individuals.

Exam tip

You should be able to show that you understand that computer systems must be reliable and robust and be able to discuss the reasons why this is important.

Check your understanding ————————————————————————— Tested

1   State the **four** essential parts of a computer system.   *(4 marks)*

2   Name **three** input devices.   *(3 marks)*

3   State **three** output devices.   *(3 marks)*

4   Explain the term computer redundancy.   *(4 marks)*

Go to page 72 for answers ————————————————————————— Checked

3.1.8.2 Hardware

Within a computer system there are basically two types of **hardware**:

● **system hardware** such as the central processing unit (CPU), which is situated on a printed circuit board called the motherboard

● other hardware such as the hard disk drive, the random access memory (RAM), optical drive and other circuit boards such as the graphics and sound cards.

> **Exam tip**
>
> You will need to be able to explain the fundamental pieces of hardware required to make a functioning computer system.
>
> You must be able to explain how developments in hardware technologies (including memory and processors) are leading to exciting innovative products being created, e.g. in the mobile and gaming industries.

3.1.8.3 CPU

A **CPU** is a type of **processor** that runs the system.

The name 'processor' is more generic but it is often used to mean the CPU. The only problem with using the term 'processor' is that there will be other processors in a computing system but only one CPU.

● The CPU undertakes instructions it receives from programs in what is called a **cycle**.

● The CPU has a number of **cores**.

● The speed of the CPU is measured in how many cycles it can perform in a second. The name given to one cycle per second is a **hertz**.

● A CPU that processes 1 million cycles per second is said to have a **clock speed** of a megahertz and a CPU that can handle 1 billion cycles per second is said to have a clock speed of one gigahertz.

> **Exam tip**
>
> You need be able to describe the purpose of the processor (CPU).
>
> You must be able to explain the concept that data and instructions are stored in memory and processed by the CPU.

↑ **Figure 8.4 A modern quad-core processor**

Mobile CPUs and processors

Mobile devices are not connected to a power socket all the time so they need a long **battery life**.

They are also small so they do not have the space for a fan to keep the CPU cool. This makes them prone to overheating.

The main differences between mobile and non-mobile processors are as follows:

- **Clock speed**: portable processors have lower clock speeds than their desktop equivalents as this lowers the amount of heat that they produce.
- The cooling requirements of any portable device require a processor that does not create too much heat.
- Space in a portable device is at a premium so most modern mobile processors also have other components integrated into the processor itself. These components often include **wireless networking components**.
- Mobile processors are **optimised** for very low power consumption.

Processing units

All computers used to have a single processor, called the **CPU**. Today many computing devices often have more than one **processing unit (PU)**. There is no single central processor for all actions.

Programmers needs to know how the CPU operates so that they can write software and understand errors.

Each **PU** in a computer system can accept the input of a **single program instruction**. The output is a result of that instruction.

Any processing unit can be divided into two other components: the **arithmetic logic unit (ALU)** and a **control unit (CU)**.

The control unit performs the following functions:

1 Fetch instructions.

2 Decode instructions.

3 Execute instructions.

4 Store results.

This four-step process is called a **processor cycle**.

Motherboard

A **motherboard** links the CPU and PUs to the memory and other hardware.

The CPU computes data and uses the motherboard to receive and send signals to components, such as the **hard drives (storage)**.

The motherboard is also responsible for holding all of the **computer settings** such as time and date.

> **Exam tip**
>
> You will need to demonstrate knowledge of the effect of common CPU characteristics on the performance of the processor. These should include clock speed, number of cores and cache size/types.

As with the CPU, motherboards have speeds, called the **bus speed**. A **bus** is the circuit that connects one part of the motherboard to another:

● The more data the motherboard bus can handle at any one time, the faster the system.

● The **speed** of the bus is measured in megahertz (MHz).

Motherboards have many buses. Each one transfers data from one computer component to another.

⬆ **Figure 8.5 A motherboard**

Graphics cards

When using programs such as computer games or 3D image editors, the **graphics card** is important.

The graphics card supports the CPU. It has a processor like the CPU. However, it is especially designed to control screen images.

The **graphics card** can be a separate circuit that slots into the computer. The advantage of this type of card is that it can be changed.

In laptops and handheld devices, the graphics card is an **integral part** of the system motherboard and cannot be changed.

The graphics card consists of two components:

● a **video chip set** that creates the signals which the screen must receive to form an image

● **random access memory (RAM)** since the video card must be able to remember a complete screen image at any time.

1   What is a CPU?   *(2 marks)*

2   Why should a CPU not be referred to simply as the processor?   *(2 marks)*

3   What does VGA mean?   *(1 mark)*

   a) video graphics array

   b) visual graphics array

   c) volatile graphics array

   d) video graphics adapter

4   What is a motherboard and why is bus speed important?   *(4 marks)*

5   CPU stands for: *(1 mark)*

   a) computer processing unit

   b) central processing unit

   c) computer protection unit

   d) central processing uploader

Go to page 72 for answers — Checked

There are two main categories of chip-based memory: **volatile** and **non-volatile**.

Volatile memory

Volatile memory is computer memory that requires a power supply in order to maintain stored data:

- The moment that the power is turned off the information is lost.
- Volatile memory is often referred to as **temporary memory**.
- The **random access memory (RAM)** in your computer is a type of volatile memory.
- Volatile memory cannot store data when the computing device is turned off.

Non-volatile memory

Non-volatile memory is computer memory that retains its information whether the power being supplied to it is turned on or switched off.

Examples of non-volatile memory include read only memory (ROM) and flash memory as well as most types of magnetic hard disks and optical disks.

How memory is used

The CPU cannot fetch the data it needs directly from the hard disk because even the slowest modern CPU processes data about 50 times faster than the fastest hard disk.

So we need fast memory and the fastest memory is **cache**.

The cache is very high-speed memory and it draws the data from the RAM as it is needed.

Cache memory

The cache is limited in size so has a limit to how much it can store.

Cache technology uses very fast but small amounts of memory to speed up slower but larger memory types.

The cache memory is taken from the **RAM** when needed.

There is no fixed cache size in a CPU but the faster the CPU, the larger the level 2 (L2) cache needs to be.

The size of the cache refers to the size of the **data store**:

- A typical L2 cache is 512 KB but can be as high as 1 MB or even2 MB.
- Within the CPU itself, level 1 (L1) cache is usually from 8 KB to 64 KB.
- The more cache memory the system has, the more likely it is to register a hit when it accesses the RAM and thus the faster it will operate.

Random access memory (RAM)

While not as fast as cache, **RAM** is fast – in fact much faster than any disk.

What this means for the user is that there is far less time waiting and more time being productive.

> **Exam tip**
>
> You must know the differences between non-volatile and volatile memory and how each is used in a system.
>
> You must be able to explain the purpose of virtual memory and cache memory.

Some graphics cards use a special memory called **Video RAM (VRAM)**:

● A VRAM cell is made up of two ordinary RAM cells which are fixed together. This double cell allows the processor to simultaneously read and write data at the same RAM address.

● RAM is **volatile**, which means that as soon as the computer is shut down – whether intentionally or by a power-cut – everything in RAM disappears.

↑ **Figure 8.6 A RAM module**

Read-only memory (ROM)

Read-only memory (ROM) doesn't forget data when it is switched off.

ROM chips have data **pre-installed** on them during manufacture. The information stored is on them permanently and can't ever be changed.

This makes ROM chips excellent for small mobile devices, where they hold the **operating system**.

Flash memory

Small portable devices, such as MP3 players, phones and cameras, need small portable memory. They use special chips called **flash memory** to store information permanently.

Flash memory has certain things in common with both ROM and RAM as it is non-volatile (it remembers information when the power is off) but it can also be erased and rewritten many times.

You also find flash memory in **memory sticks**.

Exam tip

You must understand the purpose of RAM and ROM and when each should be used.

Check your understanding ———————————————————————— Tested

1 What is the difference between volatile and non-volatile memory? *(2 marks)*

2 What is cache memory? *(3 marks)*

3 Name the main **two** types of random access memory (RAM) and state what RAM is. *(4 marks)*

4 The maximum size of main memory of a computer is determined by the: *(1 mark)*

  a) operating system

  b) address bus

  c) data bus

  d) chipset.

Go to page 73 for answers ———————————————————————— Checked

3.1.8.5 Secondary storage

Types of non-volatile secondary storage include:

- magnetic storage
- optical storage
  - compact disc (CD)
  - digital versatile disc (DVD)
  - Blu-Ray disc
- solid state disks
- USB flash drive (pen drive)
- flash memory cards.

External hard drives

External hard disk drives (HDD) are regarded as removable storage peripherals and are typically connected using a USB socket.

External HDDs are available in two formats:

- a preassembled **integrated** unit
- a unit assembled by combining an external enclosure with a **USB** or other **interface** with a separately purchased drive.

Flash drives

Flash drives are data storage devices that comprise of flash memory (a non-volatile computer storage chip that can be electrically erased and reprogrammed) coupled with an integrated USB interface.

Flash drives are removable and **rewritable** media and are conveniently small in physical size.

Optical drives

Optical drives retrieve and store data on optical discs, such as CDs, DVDs and Blu-ray discs (BDs).

Burning data to an optical disc is the most common method of copying and backing up data.

Data is burned onto the surface of an optical disc using a laser beam contained within the drive. The laser is also used to read the data from the disk.

> **Exam tip**
>
> You should be able to describe the most common types of secondary storage.
>
> You must be able to explain how optical media, magnetic media and solid state media work.

Check your understanding

Tested

1 Describe the difference between secondary storage and main memory. *(6 marks)*

2 Where do your documents exist when you are working on them in a standard software application? *(2 marks)*

Go to page 73 for answers

Checked

3.1.9 Algorithms

Every time you write a program you are creating an **algorithm**, a set of steps to perform a task.

To get a computer to do something we have to tell it what to do. We do this by using a set of instructions. These instructions are called **algorithms**:

- An algorithm has a defined outcome, a defined end.
- Algorithms can be written in many different ways. Each way has a different cost, different speed and requires different external hardware.
- In computing, an algorithm is a well-defined **procedure** that takes a value, or set of values, as input and produces an output.
- Algorithms are also used a lot in mathematics, especially in algebra.
- Algorithms are often written in words before being turned into **code**. You should write each step before attempting to create the program on the computer.

Algorithms may be divided into two groups:

- **serial algorithms**, where each step or operation is carried out in a linear order
- **parallel algorithms**, which are used with computers running parallel processors.

Exam tip

make sure you can explain how algorithms are used in computational solutions that always finish and return an answer.

You must be able to interpret simple algorithms to deduce their function.

You must be able to detect and correct errors in simple algorithms.

Exam tip

You must be able to to solve simple problems using serial and parallel algorithms.

Algorithms in file compression
Revised

All **compression** uses algorithms.

All compression algorithms are classified in computing terms as either **lossless** or **lossy**:

- Lossless algorithms do not change the content of a file. They are used to compress text and program files.
- Lossy algorithms achieve better **compression** by selectively deleting some of the information in the file. These algorithms are used for large images or sound files but not for text or program data. The **JPEG** and **MP3** compression algorithms are lossy.

Algorithms in security
Revised

If you program anything that works over the internet and needs to handle confidential information, you will have to use **cryptographic algorithms** to keep the system secure.

Cryptographic algorithms are sequences of rules that are used to **encrypt and decipher** code.

Most security algorithms involve the use of encryption, which allows two parties to communicate but uses coded messages so that third parties such as hackers cannot understand the communications.

Encryption algorithms are used to transform plain text into something unreadable.

The encrypted data is then decrypted to restore it, making it understandable to the intended recipient.

There are hundreds of different types of cryptographic algorithms, but most fit into two classifications, they are either **symmetric** or **asymmetric**:

● Asymmetric algorithms use two keys – a **public key** and a **private key**. The public key can be shared, but, to protect the data, the private key is only stored by the user. **Encryption** and **decryption** of data needs both private and public keys.

● Symmetric algorithms are faster than asymmetric algorithms as one key is required. The disadvantage of this system is that both parties know the **secret key**.

Check your understanding   Tested

1   Briefly describe the term 'algorithm'.   *(1 mark)*

2   How can algorithms be represented?   *(1 mark)*

3   Write an algorithm that can find the maximum of *N* values entered into a computer.   *(6 marks)*

4   Write an algorithm that can find the sum and product of *N* values.   *(6 marks)*

Go to page 74 for answers   Checked

3.1.10 Data representation

Differences between **digital** and **analogue** data:

- **Analogue data** is continuous, analogous to the actual information it represents. For example, a mercury thermometer is an analogue device: the mercury rises in direct proportion to the temperature.

- Computers cannot work with analogue information.

- **Digital data** breaks the analogue information into separate, discrete steps and represents those pieces using **binary digits**.

Bits, nibbles and bytes

Revised

- A **bit** has a value of 1 or 0.
- A **nibble** is four bits.
- A **byte** is eight bits.

Because a bit is so small we can't use a bit as the comparison for the next section of our list.

- A kilobyte (KB) is 1024 bytes.
- A megabyte (MB) is 1 048 576 bytes or (it is easier to remember) 1024 kilobytes.
- A gigabyte (GB) is 1024 megabytes or 1 048 576 kilobytes.
- A terabyte (TB) is 1024 gigabytes or 1 048 576 megabytes.
- A petabyte (PB) is 1024 terabytes or 1 048 576 gigabytes.
- An exabyte (EB) is 1024 petabytes or 1 048 576 terabytes.
- A zettabyte (ZB) is 1024 exabytes or 1 048 576 petabytes.
- A yottabyte (YB) is 1024 zettabytes or 1 048 576 exabytes.

Representing sound data

Revised

The **MP3** file format was designed to encode a raw audio file as a sequence of 0s and 1s.

Sound is stored according to sample rates. The higher the **sample rate** the better the quality but the larger the **file size**.

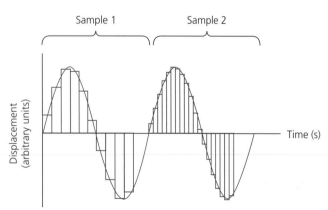

↑ **Figure 10.1 Digitising an analogue sound wave**

Representing image data

- We can use a **two-dimensional data array** to define an image.
- Think about the **pixels** in a digital photograph.
- The larger the number of pixels the larger the file size but higher the **image quality**.

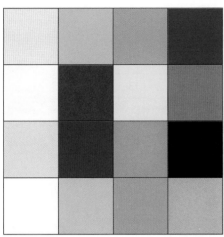

↑ Figure 10.2 A colour photograph's pixels viewed close up

Representing text using ASCII

ASCII stands for **American Standard Code for Information Interchange**.

The **ASCII** standard associates a seven-bit binary number with each of 128 distinct characters:

	000	001	010	011	100	101	110	111
0000	NULL	DLE		0	@	P	`	p
0001	SOH	DC1	!	1	A	Q	a	q
0010	STX	DC2	"	2	B	R	b	r
0011	ETX	DC3	#	3	C	S	c	s
0100	EDT	DC4	$	4	D	T	d	t
0101	ENQ	NAK	%	5	E	U	e	u
0110	ACK	SYN	&	6	F	V	f	v
0111	BEL	ETB	'	7	G	W	g	w
1000	BS	CAN	(	8	H	X	h	x
1001	HT	EM	)	9	I	Y	i	y
1010	LF	SUB	*	:	J	Z	j	z
1011	VT	ESC	+	;	K	[	k	{
1100	FF	FS	,	<	L	\	l		
1101	CR	GS	-	=	M	]	m	}
1110	SO	RS	.	>	N	^	n	~
1111	SI	US	/	?	O	_	o	DEL

As we have seen computers can only understand numbers, so an ASCII code is the numerical representation of a character, such as from 'a' to 'z' or '@', or even an action of some sort (e.g. DEL).

Exam tip

Make sure you can explain how characters are represented in binary and are familiar with ASCII and its limitations.

Hexadecimal numbers

There are **16 hexadecimal digits**.

They look exactly the same as the decimal digits up to 9 but then there are the letters A, B, C, D, E and F in place of the **denary** numbers 10 to 15.

A single hexadecimal digit can show **16 different values** instead of the decimal 10, like this:

Decimal	0	1	2	3	4	5	6	7	8	9	10	11	12	13	14	15
Hexadecimal	0	1	2	3	4	5	6	7	8	9	A	B	C	D	E	F

Converting **hexadecimal** numbers is much harder than converting **binary** numbers.

Remember the following facts to help you:

  You always work backwards to convert these numbers.

  Any number to the **power** of 0 equals 1.

  We write powers in computing using ^ so 16 to the power of 3 is written as 16^3.

The following table shows the first five powers of 16:

Powers of 16	Calculation	Result
16^0		1
16^1	16	16
16^2	16 × 16	256
16^3	16 × 16 × 16	4096
16^4	16 × 16 × 16 × 16	65536

If we have a hexadecimal number of 1128, its denary value is calculated as follows:

  The last digit is 8. It represents $8 \times (16^0) = 8$.

  The next digit is 2. This represents $2 \times (16^1) = 2 \times 16 = 32$.

  The next digit is 1. This is $1 \times (16^2) = 1 \times 256 = 256$.

  The final digit is 1. This is $1 \times (16^3) = 1 \times 4096 = 4096$.

  If we add the totals together 1128 in hexadecimal
  = 4096 + 256 + 32 + 8 = 4392 in denary.

You may be asking about the letters. They work the same way, so FA8 is calculated as:

  $8 \times 1 = 8$

  $10 \times 16 = 160$ (remember A = 10 and this has to be multiplied by 16^1)

  $15 \times 256 = 3840$ (remember F = 15 and this has to be multiplied by 16^2)

  The total in denary is 3840 + 160 + 8 = 4008.

Exam tip

You need to be able to explain why hexadecimal number representation is often used and know how to convert between binary, denary and hexadecimal.

You must be able to explain how binary can be used to represent positive whole numbers (up to 255).

Programming languages

- A high-level language is a language for programming computers which does not require detailed knowledge of a specific type of computer. To use a low-level language, the programmer does need this knowledge.

- A low-level language is a computer programming language that is closer to machine language.

- Machine language is at the lowest level, because this is the actual binary code that the computer understands.

Programs in a high-level language do not have to be written for a particular computer. They have to be compiled into machine code for the computer they will run on.

High-level languages are much easier for humans to understand than low-level languages. They usually include command statements, such as WHILE or FOR, which are regular English words.

Check your understanding   Tested

1 1 kilobyte refers to: (1 mark)

   a) 1000 bytes

   b) 1024 bytes

   c) 8000 bytes

   d) 8192 bytes

2 Give the **four** main differences between low-level and high-level
   programming.   (4 marks)

3 Convert the denary number 1792 to binary.   (1 mark)

4 What meat do you get if you convert the denary number 48879
   to hexadecimal?   (2 marks)

Go to page 74 for answers   Checked

3.1.11 Software development life cycle

The software **development life cycle** is a structured procedure used for developing software products.

It describes the steps, called **phases**, of the software cycle and the order in which those phases are carried out.

It is sometimes referred to as the **software life cycle** or **software process**.

It is an important part of the larger **systems development life cycle**.

There are a number of models that offer different approaches to the variety of phases that occur during the whole cycle and some software development organisations adopt their own but all have very similar patterns.

The basic model is shown in Figure 11.1.

<table>
<tr><td>

Exam tip

You must be able to explain the software development life cycle and what commonly occurs at each stage of the software development life cycle.

</td></tr>
</table>

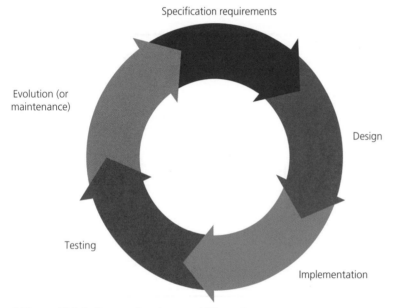

↑ **Figure 11.1 Software development life cycle**

Design stage   Revised ☐

This is where the details on how the software will work are created.

You normally do it using a **flowchart**, before programming anything.

This stage often includes the design of the 'look and feel' of the **software interface** too.

Implementation stage   Revised ☐

From the deliverables that come out of the **design phase**, code is written during the **implementation stage**.

This is usually the longest phase of the software development life cycle.

For a developer, this phase is the main focus of the life cycle because this is where the code is produced.

There is the possibility that the implementation stage may overlap with both the design and testing phases.

The code is written from the designs, testing and improving it as it is developed.

Testing stage

During the **testing phase**, the implementation is tested against the specification requirements to ensure that the product is actually providing a solution to the needs addressed and gathered during the **requirements phase**.

Certain tests such as unit tests and software acceptance tests are carried out during this phase.

Unit tests focus on a specific component of the software, while **software tests** act on the program as a whole.

Evolution (or maintenance) stage

Even the best software products undergo changes or **upgrades** once they are delivered to the customer.

There can be a number of different reasons why these changes can happen, such as a consequence of some unexpected input values into the software.

It is imperative that the software be developed to accommodate changes that could happen during the **post-implementation period**.

Exam tip

You must be able to identify at which stage of the software development life cycle a given step would occur.

Types of life cycle model

Waterfall model

This is by far the most common of the life cycle models. It is sometimes referred to as a **linear-sequential life cycle model**.

In a **waterfall software development model**, each phase must be totally completed prior to the next phase beginning. Phases do not overlap.

At the end of each of the phases, reviews are carried out to determine if the project is proceeding correctly and a decision is made as to whether the project should be continued or discarded.

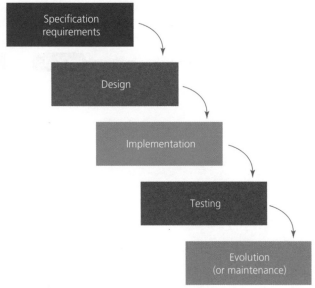

↑ **Figure 11.2 Waterfall life cycle model**

The advantages of the waterfall model are:

- It is simple and easy to use.
- It is easy to manage due to the rigidity of the model – each phase has specific deliverables and a review process.
- Phases are processed and completed one at a time.
- It works well for smaller projects where requirements are very well understood.

The disadvantages of the waterfall model are:

- Adjusting what is wanted during the life cycle can kill a project, i.e. there is a lack of flexibility.
- No working software is produced until late in the life cycle.
- There are high amounts of risk and uncertainty.

It is a poor model for complex and object-oriented projects or for long and ongoing projects.

It is a poor model where requirements are at a moderate to high risk of changing.

Exam tip

You must be able to explain several life cycle models that can be used (e.g. cyclical, waterfall, spiral).

Incremental model

The **incremental model** is similar to the waterfall model.

Within this model, more than one development cycle occurs at the same time, making this life cycle a kind of 'multi-waterfall' cycle.

Cycles are divided up into smaller, more easily managed **iterations** and each iteration passes through the requirements, design, testing and implementation phases.

A working version of software is produced during the **first build**, resulting in working software being available early on during the software life cycle.

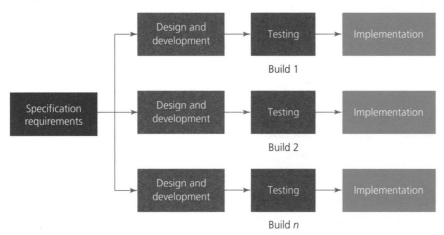

↑ **Figure 11.3 Incremental life cycle model**

Advantages of the incremental model include:

- It produces working software quickly and early on during the software life cycle.
- It is a more flexible model – it is less costly to change scope and requirements.
- It is easier to test and debug during a smaller iteration.
- It is easier to manage risk because risky pieces are identified and handled during their iterations.
- Each iteration is an easily managed milestone.

Disadvantages of the incremental model include:

- Each phase of an iteration is rigid and does not overlap any other.
- Problems associated with software architecture could arise due to not all of the requirements being gathered upfront for the entire software life cycle.

Spiral model

The **spiral model** places emphasis on risk analysis and has four phases:

- planning
- risk analysis
- engineering
- evaluation.

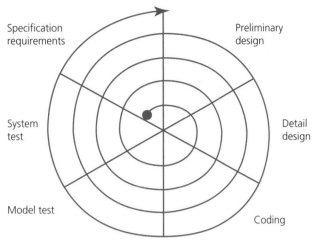

Specification requirements

Preliminary design

System test

Detail design

Model test

Coding

↑ **Figure 11.4 The spiral life cycle model**

The software project repeatedly passes through each of the phases in iterations, which are called 'spirals':

1 Within the **baseline spiral**, which commences in the **planning (preliminary design) phase** requirements are gathered and the risk is assessed. Each subsequent spiral builds on the baseline spiral.

2 During the planning phase, the design requirements are gathered.

3 In the **risk analysis (design detail) phase** a process is undertaken to identify risk and alternative solutions. A **prototype** is then produced at the end of the risk analysis phase.

4 The actual software is produced within the **engineering (coding) phase** and tested at the end of the phase.

5 The **evaluation (testing) phase** allows the customer to evaluate the output of the project to date before the project continues to the next spiral.

In the spiral model, the **angular component** represents progress and the **radius** of the spiral represents cost.

Advantages of the spiral model include:

It has a high degree of risk analysis.

It is an excellent model for large and mission-critical projects.

Software is produced early within the software life cycle.

Disadvantages of the spiral model include:

It can be a costly model to adopt.

Risk analysis requires highly specific expertise.

The project's success is highly dependent on the risk analysis phase.

It is not an appropriate choice for smaller projects.

V-shaped model

Similar to the waterfall model, the **V-shaped model** follows a sequential path of task execution and it is important that each phase is completed before the next phase commences.

The high-level design phase focuses on **software architecture** and design. An **integration test plan** is also created in this phase with the purpose of testing the ability of the separate pieces of software to work together.

The **low-level design phase** (the detailed specification phase) is where the actual software components are designed and unit tests are produced.

Just as in the waterfall model, the implementation phase is where all coding takes place. Once coding is complete, the sequence of execution continues up the right side of the 'V' where the test plans developed earlier are now utilised.

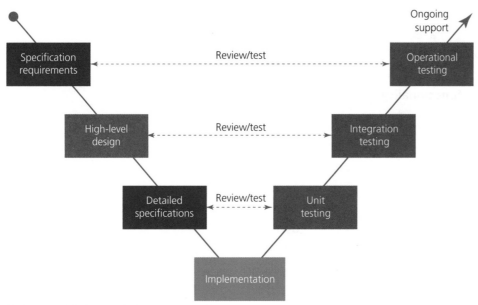

↑ **Figure 11.5 V-shaped life cycle model**

The advantages of the V-shaped model are:

- It is simple and easy to use.
- Each phase has specific deliverables.
- There is a higher chance of success than in the waterfall model as a consequence of the development of test plans early on during the life cycle.
- It works well for small projects where requirements are easily understood.

The disadvantages of the V-shaped model are:

- It is very rigid, in a similar way to the waterfall model.
- There is little flexibility and adjusting scope is difficult and expensive.
- Software is developed during the implementation phase, so no early prototypes of the software are produced.
- The model doesn't provide a clear path for problems found during testing phases.

Exam tip

You must be able to describe and discuss the advantages and disadvantages of different life cycle models.

Check your understanding   Tested

1 What are the **five** main stages in a software development life cycle?   *(5 marks)*

2 What happens during the testing phase?   *(2 marks)*

3 List **three** advantages and **two** disadvantages of the spiral model.   *(5 marks)*

Go to page 75 for answers   Checked

3.1.11.1 Prototyping

What is prototyping?

The concept behind prototyping is to offer people the capability of **evaluating** the system developer's proposed designs, rather than having to interpret those designs based on some other means such as descriptions.

A **prototype** typically simulates only a few aspects of the final product and at this point may be completely different from the end result.

The most useful purpose of prototyping is based upon providing a simulation of some behaviour or **functionality**.

Advantages of prototyping

Prototyping offers many advantages within software development.

- It allows the customer and the developer to compare if the developed software matches the **software specification** according to which the program should have been built.

- It can offer improvements to the quality and definition of **customer requirements** and improve the specifications provided to developers.

- Making a **functioning** (or even a **non-functioning**) prototype first often results in faster and less expensive software and less wasted time.

- A fundamental requirement of prototyping is **end-user involvement**. The users can see and interact with a prototype providing them with an opportunity to offer improved and more thorough **feedback** and specifications.

- The existence of a prototype enabling detailed examination by users prevents the misunderstandings and miscommunications that can occur when each side thinks the other understands what they said.

- Since users understand the fundamental issues of the problem better than anyone on the development team, the increased interaction can contribute to a final product that is more likely to satisfy the users' desire for look, feel and performance.

Disadvantages of prototyping

Prototyping can also have disadvantages although this can often be put down to misusing the process of prototyping:

- If a limited prototype is the focus, developers can be distracted from properly analysing the complete project.

- Prototypes are limited in functionality and may not scale well if they are used as the basis for a final product.

- Users can begin to think that a prototype, which is intended to be discarded, is actually the final system.

- Users can become attached to functionality that was included in a prototype for consideration and then removed from the specification for the final system; this can lead to conflict.

- Developers may spend a great deal of effort producing the prototype and may attempt to convert a limited prototype into a final system when it does not have an appropriate underlying architecture.

- Prototyping is supposed to be carried out quickly; if developers lose sight of this fact, they may try to develop a prototype that is too complex.

- Prototyping is expensive:

  - The startup costs for constructing a development team that is focused on prototyping may be high.

  - There may be a high expectation of productivity without sufficient focus on the learning curve in using the prototyping technology.

  - Training on the prototyping technique and the requirement to develop corporate and project-specific support for the technology is often overlooked; as a consequence, only low productivity is achieved.

Check your understanding   Tested

1 What is prototyping and what is its purpose?   (4 marks)

2 State **three** advantages and **four** disadvantages of prototyping.   (7 marks)

Go to page 76 for answers   Checked

3.1.12 Application testing

Application testing is much more than just **error detection**.

Testing software means operating the software under **controlled conditions** to see how well it works.

To accurately test a solution you must have a good clear specification before you start the design phase of a project.

There are two reasons to test:

Testing verifies that the application meets the **specification criteria** that was agreed between the developer and the **client**.

Testing manages risk for both client and the developer.

- A **testing programme** identifies whether an application has been produced to the specified requirements of both the client and developer so that the programmers' work can be ended and paid for.

- The project then shifts into the **maintenance** part of the software development life cycle.

Test plans and test strategies

Revised

Test plans and **test strategies** are not the same documents.

A **test plan** should be developed with each program. The test plan says how you intend to test the program. Only measurable things should be included in a test plan. Another document is produced showing the results of these tests.

A **test strategy** contains an account of the testing approach for a software development life cycle. It informs project managers and developers about a range of key issues related to the testing process, including the testing objectives, methods of testing new functionality, details of the total testing time and a description of the requirements for resources for the testing environment.

A typical test strategy document of a software company could include:

the scope and objectives: what exactly is required?

the roles and responsibilities: who is responsible for what?

communication and status reporting: how will communication take place, when and in what format (e.g. reports)?

test deliverability: what tests will take place and against what standards?

industry standards: what rules and standards will be followed?

test automation and tools: how will the tests take place and using which tools?

testing measurements and metrics: what measurements will be taken?

defect reporting and tracking: how will faults found be recorded and corrected?

change and configuration management: what happens if a change is required?

training plan: how will end users be trained to use the product, e.g. product manuals needed etc.?

Test strategies usually give an account of how risks for the company relative to an application are lessened by carrying out the tests.

They also provide a list of the kind of tests that will be performed and what entry and exit criteria (if any) will apply:

● Under **normal** conditions: The application is tested under normal working conditions and the data that the coded solution is supplied with is within the anticipated range.

Under **extreme** conditions: The coded solution is provided with data that is within the operating range but at its limits of performance.

Error behaviour: An application or program is provided with data that is outside of its limits of performance. The tests try to break the application and to investigate if things occur when they shouldn't or vice versa.

Verification and validation

Revised

Within software development, testing is always carried out along with procedures of **verification** and **validation**:

● **Verification** is the testing of whether the software performs against criteria that are decided in advance.

Validation is when we check that an application has been correctly written against a specification that has been agreed with the customer.

Defining test criteria

Revised

When writing a test plan, there are a variety of methods that can be used for differing testing scenarios.

Pass/fail criteria

When developers carry out tests on code, it is inevitable that some aspects will pass and some will fail.

The pass/fail criteria need to be described in clear, unambiguous language and agreed with the client.

A process should be defined in advance of the tests to allow the developers to record the problems that occur and also any other issues they think need sorting out.

Pass/fail criteria are sometimes referred to as entry/exit or compliance criteria.

It is common for pass/fail test criteria to be utilised in the testing of **graphical user interfaces** (GUIs).

Acceptance criteria

Acceptance testing is a validation test that is carried out to judge whether the requirements of specific criteria or a whole contract have been successfully achieved.

The acceptance criteria should be clearly defined and agreed upon between the client and the developer.

Acceptance criteria test methods should also be defined and agreed.

Non-functional testing

Non-functional testing tends to reflect the quality of the product, particularly the suitability of the application from the point of view of the client.

The non-functional testing of applications tends to look at the application as a whole:

● A **load test** investigates software behaviour during increasing system loads (for instance, the number of users that use a piece of software simultaneously).

● A **performance test** investigates the processing speed and response time for specific scenarios, usually associated with increasing load.

Unit/modular testing

Unit testing, which is also referred to as **component testing**, is a software development process where the small parts of an application, called **units**, are individually and independently looked at to see if they work correctly.

Unit testing is often automated but it can also be done manually.

Unit testing is part of a method of software development that takes a detailed approach to building a product by means of continual testing and revision.

Developers usually create unit tests as they work on code to ensure that the specific function is working as expected.

Commonly, one function of the application might have multiple tests, to catch certain errors within the code.

Unit testing alone cannot verify the functionality of an application; it is a method of assuring that the building blocks that the program utilises work independently of each other.

Alpha tests

Alpha testing is commonly applied to **off-the-shelf applications** and is regularly used as a kind of internal acceptance testing procedure before to the program is sent for beta testing.

Beta tests

Beta testing comes after alpha testing and is viewed as a type of **external user acceptance testing**.

A version of the application is released to a limited group of users who are independent of the development team.

> **Exam tip**
>
> You must be able to explain the different types of tests that can be used, including unit/modular testing.

Check your understanding | Tested

1 Why is testing important? *(2 marks)*

Go to page 76 for answers | Checked

3.1.13 Networking

Definition of a computer network

A computer network can be described as two or more computers connected together through a communication medium to form a network.

The purpose of connecting computers together in a network is to exchange information and data. Networked computers can also use the resources of other computers on the network.

Advantages of computer networks include:

- Networks allow users to share software stored in a main system. **Site (network) software licenses** are less expensive than buying several **standalone** licenses.

- Files can easily be shared between users over a network.

- Network users can communicate via email, instant messenger and VoIP.

- Security over networks is of a high standard, i.e. users cannot see other users' files unlike on standalone machines used by several users.

- Within networks, it is much more straightforward to **back up data** as it is all stored on a **file server**.

- Networks allow data to be transmitted to remote areas that are connected within local areas.

- Networked computers allow users to share common **peripheral resources**, such as printers, fax machines and modems, therefore saving money.

- The cost of computing is reduced per user as compared to the development and maintenance of a group of standalone computers.

Disadvantages of computer networks include:

- Cabling to construct a network and **file servers** can be costly.

- The management of a large network is complicated. It requires training and a **specialist network manager** usually needs to be employed.

- In the event of a file server breaking down, the files contained on the server become inaccessible, although email might still work if it is stored on a separate **email server**. The computers can still be used but are isolated.

- If a **virus** gets into the system, it can easily spread through the network to other computers.

- With networks, particularly **wide area networks**, there is a risk of hacking. Stringent security measures, such as a **firewall**, are required to prevent such abuse.

> **Exam tip**
>
> You will need to be able to discuss the advantages and disadvantages of using a computer network.

Basic components of a computer network

- **Servers** are powerful computers that provide services to the other computers on the network.

- **Clients** are computers that use the services that a server provides. Clients are usually less powerful than the server although even the largest **mainframe** in the world can act as a client to a small **web server** somewhere in the world.

- **Communication media** consists of the **physical connections** between the devices on a network. This could be through cable in an organisation's local network, a **wireless signal** or the internet.

- A **network adapter** or, as it's often referred to, a **network interface card (NIC)** is a circuit board that is equipped with the components necessary for sending and receiving data. It is usually plugged into one of the available slots on a computer and a transmission cable is attached to the connector on the NIC.

- The **resources** mean any **peripheral device** that is available to a client on the network such as a printer, a fax device or other network devices; however, the term also refers to **data and information**.

- A **user** is basically any person that uses a client to access resources on the network.

- The **protocols** of a network are formal, written rules used for the network communications. They are essentially the languages that computers use to communicate on a network.

Network topologies

Bus topology

Bus networks use a common backbone to connect all devices.

A single cable that functions as the **backbone** of the network acts as a shared communication medium that devices connect to via an interface connector.

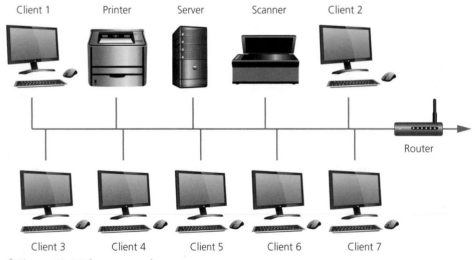

↑ **Figure 13.1 A bus network**

The advantages of the bus topology are:

● It is easy and cheap to install as a consequence of requiring only a small quantity of cable.

● It is suitable for small networks.

The disadvantages of the bus topology are:

● The cable length is limited. This restricts the number of devices that can be connected to the network.

● As more devices are connected, the performance of the network becomes slower as a consequence of data collisions.

Ring topology

When every device has exactly two neighbours for communication purposes, the network layout is referred to as a **ring network**.

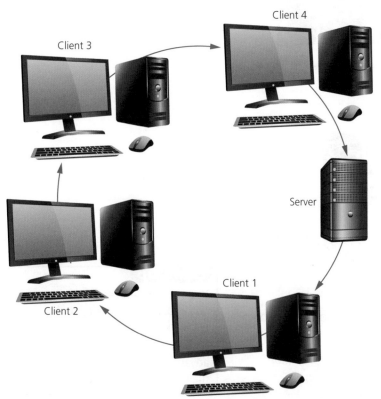

↑ **Figure 13.2 A ring network**

In the ring topology, all messages pass around in the same direction. This can be either clockwise or anticlockwise.

Ring topologies are found in some office buildings or school campuses.

The advantage of the ring topology is that a central server is not required – messages sent between two workstations pass through all the intermediate devices.

The disadvantages of the ring topology are:

● The failure of any cable within the network or of any device can cause the entire network to crash.

● Alterations or maintenance to the network nodes can impact the performance of the whole network.

Star topology

Nearly all home networks use the **star topology**.

The star network has a central connection point referred to as a **hub node**. It could be a device such as **network hub**, a **switch** or a **router**.

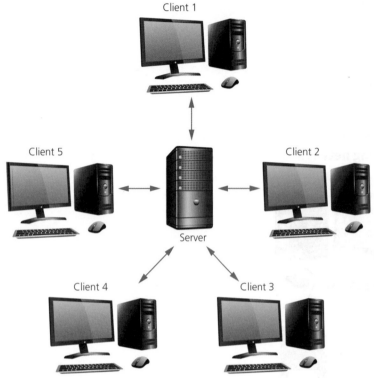

Client 1

Client 5

Client 2

Server

Client 4

Client 3

↑ **Figure 13.3 A star network**

Star networks generally require more cable than bus topologies.

The advantages of the star topology are:

● operational simplicity, as a consequence of its centralised layout

● the possibility of isolating each device within the network, so changes to one do not affect others.

The disadvantage of the star topology is that the network operation ultimately relies on the correct functioning of the central hub. If the central hub crashes, it leads to failure of the whole network.

> **Exam tip**
>
> You must be able to describe and explain the bus, ring and star networking topologies.
>
> Make sure you can discuss the advantages and disadvantages of the main types of network topology.

Wireless networks
Revised

A wireless (WiFi) network and a **portable personal router (MyFi)** use radio waves to communicate. Radios, mobile phones and televisions also use radio waves.

↑ **Figure 13.4 A wireless network**

This is what happens:

1 A computer's **wireless adapter** translates data into a radio signal and transmits it using an antenna; it receives radio signals and converts them into data.

2 A wireless modem called a **router** (WiFi and MyFi) handles the two-way communication.

3 The router is usually connected by a physical, **ethernet connection**, but MyFi uses wireless networks to connect to the internet servers.

Check your understanding   Tested

1 What is a computer network and why is it useful? *(4 marks)*

2 What is a network client? *(2 marks)*

3 The number of bits that can be transmitted over a network in a certain period of time is: *(1 mark)*

   a) delay time

   b) latency rate

   c) bandwidth

   d) baud rate

4 A technique in which system resources are shared among multiple users is: *(1 mark)*

   a) multiplexing

   b) modulation

   c) demultiplexing

   d) demodulation

5 List five advantages and five disadvantages of using computer networks. *(10 marks)*

Go to page 76 for answers   Checked

3.1.13.1 Client–server

The **client–server model** is the structure of a computer network in which many clients (remote processors) request and receive services from a **centralised server** (the host computer).

Within any network, the client–server model is a very efficient way of connecting applications that are **distributed** effectively across different locations:

- Client computers provide an **interface** to allow a computer user to request services of the server and to display the results the server returns on the client.

- Servers wait for requests to arrive from clients and then respond to them.

- Clients need not be aware of the specifics of the system (i.e., the hardware and software) that is providing the service.

Handshaking

For computers to work together they have to use **protocols**.

- A protocol is a set of rules which governs the **transfer of data** between computers.

- Protocols are essential for any communication between computers and networks. They determine the speed of transmission, size of bytes, error checking methods, and even whether communication will be asynchronous or synchronous.

When two computers first connect in a network they use a **handshake**.

- Handshaking establishes which protocols to use and controls the flow of data between the two or more connected computers.

- During handshaking, the **protocol parameters** are **negotiated**.

- All network connections, such as a request from a web browser to a web server, or a file-sharing connection between **peer-to-peer** computers, have their own **handshaking protocols**, which must be completed before finishing the action requested by the user.

- The handshaking process usually occurs when a computer is about to communicate with a **foreign device** to establish the rules for communication.

> **Exam tip**
> You must be able to explain the handshake process used in most modern networking protocols.

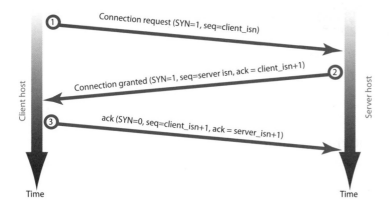

Exam tip

You must be able to explain how coding for a client–server model is different from coding for a standalone application.

Make sure you can explain the concept of coding at both the server and the client end.

1. A request to connect in sent
2. A connection in granted
3. Protocol parameters are greed

Differences between client-side and server-side programming

- **Client-side programming** is run on the client machine. An example of a client-side programming language is **Javascript**.

- **Server-side programming** is run on the **remote server**. Some examples of server-side programming languages are **PHP**, **C#** and **.NET**.

Check your understanding — Tested ☐

1 What is a protocol and a handshake when referring to computer networks? *(4 marks)*

2 What are the **five** basic needs of a networked communication system? *(5 marks)*

Go to page 77 for answers — Checked ☐

When you go onto the internet, you are using a **client–server network**.

When you see web pages displayed in your **browser**, they are on your own computer or mobile device:

○ The pages are stored on a **web server**, located anywhere in the world.

○ The **web browser** is on your own computer. It **interprets code** that is sent to it from the web server and turns it into a web page.

○ The code is mainly **HTML** but will probably also contain elements of **Javascript**, **Flash movies** and more.

○ PHP is a **server-side programming language**; it runs on the server, not on your machine.

○ PHP can be run within HTML and can also contain **Javascript code**.

Advantages and disadvantages of a client–server model

The advantages of a client–server network are:

○ Everything is centralised and managed in one place.

○ Access rights and resource allocation are all done by **servers**.

○ All the files are stored at the same place; in this way, finding files and file management is easy.

○ **Back up** and **recovery** are much simpler and often automatic.

○ Updates, new resources and systems can be added by making necessary changes in the server.

○ The server can be accessed remotely across different devices.

○ As new information is uploaded to a **server database**, each workstation does not need to have its own storage capacities increased.

○ **Server-side security** is much more robust.

The disadvantages of a client–server network are:

○ Too many requests from the clients may lead to **congestion in the network**.

● If you are downloading a file from a server and it gets abandoned due to some error, the download stops altogether.

○ It is very expensive to install and manage this type of computing.

○ You need professional IT people to maintain the servers and network.

Some of the disadvantages of client–server networks become advantages in a **cloud-based network** where maintenance is externally provided and costs of installation reduce significantly.

What is done server side?

○ One of the main functions that requires **server-side code** is to build pages customised for the type of browser that requested a page. Movies, for example, require different versions according to the browser being used.

○ Server-side code can also draw information from a **database** to create information for a web page.

○ Anything that requires information from a database, such as the number of people on the server, their address and any type of analytical information has to be done on the **server side**.

- A visitor counter is usually a server-side program.
- As internet speeds get faster and more reliable, counters can use client-side scripting using **JQuery** which runs on the client side but accesses a database on the server side.
- Web programmers like server-side scripts, such as PHP, as they are more secure than client-side code. You can't download and steal the code if it is server side.

What is done client side?

Client-side programming is important because the client and the server are not always connected. The browser is separate from the **server**:

- By including code within the web page, a number of **features** can be added.
- This is also a much quicker way to execute code even if the client and server are connected as the communications between parts of your computer are much faster than any internet connection.
- **HTML, Flash files, Javascript, ActiveX** control, and a number of other technologies can be executed on the client side. You can execute any technology supported by your browser.

> **Exam tip**
> You must be able to explain what can be coded at the client end.

Security

Server-side coded scripts are much more secure than **client-side scripts**.

Many web-based games run on the server side for the same reason: the programmer needs to make sure players cannot modify the data and hack into the game code.

Web applications

A web application is a server-side application that can be used by accessing a web server through the internet or an **intranet**. The browser is used as a **thin client**.

This type of application has become very popular due to the ability of the programmers to update and maintain web applications without the end user needing to update the software on their own machines.

> **Exam tip**
> You must have experience of coding solutions to simple web application problems.

Check your understanding   Tested

1 List **five** advantages and **three** disadvantages of a client–server model.   *(8 marks)*

Go to page 77 for answers   Checked

3.1.14 Use of external code sources

Web mashups Revised

A **web mashup** is simply a web page or coded application used to combine data or functionality from two or more sources to create a new product.

An **Application Programming Interface (API)** allows developers to integrate, for example, mapping into their own applications without developing all the mapping code themselves.

Programmers can now integrate code from these external sources into their own code. They simply use external code, web feeds, JavaScript and widgets. There are APIs for a multitude of uses, including Flickr, Yahoo, YouTube, PayPal, Twitter, Facebook, price comparison tools for online shopping and multi-site searches.

> **Exam tip**
>
> You should be able to explain the use of external code sources and how to integrate code from these sources into your own code.

What is IFrame? Revised

- An **IFrame (Inline Frame)** is an HTML document embedded inside another HTML document on a website.

- An IFrame is used to embed content from another source into a web page.

- An IFrame can be configured with its own scrollbar independent of the surrounding page's scrollbar.

- To the user they are still on the same site but in reality they have embedded content and programming from another source. The user does not have to reload the surrounding page.

- IFrames often use JavaScript but they are designed to embed interactive applications in web pages which can be either client or server side.

What is an API? Revised

- API stands for **Application Programming Interface**. The key word is **interface**.

- An interface is a common boundary between two separate systems. It is the way that code on two different systems can communicate with each other.

- APIs are carefully coded to expose only chosen functionality and data to third parties who want to use the external functionality and code. They have to safeguard other parts of the application.

- APIs are invisible to the end user – they run silently in the background.

- They provide a channel for applications to work with each other to make sure the client gets the required functionality and information.

Check your understanding

Tested

1 What is a mashup? (2 marks)

2 What is an IFrame? (2 marks)

3 What is an API? (2 marks)

Go to page 78 for answers

Checked

3.1.15 Database concepts

All businesses have data that needs to be gathered, collated and analysed and a **relational database** satisfies these requirements.

↑ **Figure 15.1 Relational databases can be used to look after business data.**

Databases use a series of **tables** to store the data:

- A table simply refers to a two-dimensional representation of data stored in **rows** and **columns**.
- A **flat file database** has only one table.
- A **relational database** has several tables linked together.

A **relational database** is a group of data items assembled into a set of formatted tables from which data can be searched, accessed and interrogated in a multitude of different ways without having to reorganise the database tables:

- Each table needs a unique name so that the **database management system** (often referred to as a DBMS) can find the right table.
- The standard user interface to any relational database is the **structured query language (SQL)**.
- By using **SQL statements**, interactive queries for information can be made for the purpose of retrieving information from a relational database and for gathering data for reports.
- A relational database has the significant benefit over a flat file database of being relatively straightforward to **extend**.

Exam tip

You will need to demonstrate understanding of the basic concepts of a relational database as a data store.

Components of relational databases

The foundation for any **relational database management system (RDBMS)** is the relational model and this has three basic components:

- a store
- a method of creating and retrieving data
- a method of ensuring that the data is logically consistent.

Tables

- A **table** in a relational database is also referred to as a 'relation'.
- It is a **two-dimensional** structure used to store related information.
- A relational database consists of two or more related tables.

Records

- A record is a complete single set of information.
- Records are comprised of fields.
- A set of records constitutes a file.

Rows

- A **row** within a relation (table) is an instance of one record.

Columns

- A **column** within a database table contains all the information of a single type.
- As part of the **validation** and **verification** of the information, columns are usually formatted to accept certain types of data such as integers, Booleans, decimals (to a stated number of decimal places) or strings.

Fields

- A **field** is a single snippet of data that is at the intersection of a row and a column.
- It is the smallest piece of information that can be retrieved using the database's **structured query language** (SQL) and forms part of an individual record.

Queries

- A database **query** is fundamentally a question that you put to the database.
- The outcome of the query is the information that is returned by the database in answer to the question.
- Queries are created using **SQL (structured query language)**, which looks like a high-level programming language.

Primary keys

- Every table in a relational database should contain one or more columns that are assigned as the **primary key**.
- The important and crucial fact for the primary key to work is that the value it holds must be unique for each of the records contained within the table.

Relationships

● Database **relationships** work by comparing data in key fields.

● This occurs between fields that have corresponding names in linked tables.

● In almost all cases, the fields contain the **primary key** for one of the tables, which then supplies the unique identifier for each record and the 'foreign' key in the other table.

● The foreign key is a column identified to establish a **connection** between the data in two tables.

● A link is established between two tables by adding the column that holds the primary key in the first table to the other table. The duplicated column within the second table then becomes the **foreign key**.

Exam tip

You must be able to explain the terms record, field, table, query, primary key, relationship, index and search criteria.

3.1.15.1 Query methods (SQL)
Revised

All **SQL code** is written in the form of a query statement and this is 'executed' against a database.

SQL queries perform some type of data operation which could be selecting, inserting/updating, or creating what are called **data objects**.

Every query statement begins with a clause such as `DELETE`, `CREATE`, `SELECT` or `UPDATE`.

SQL databases can be created on a single machine but often large databases are shared between users. This is achieved by installing them on a **dedicated server**.

Exam tip

Make sure you can create simple SQL statements to extract, add and edit data stored in databases.

You must know how to use SQL statements within your own coded systems.

3.1.15.2 Connecting to databases from applications and web-based apps
Revised

Web-based databases are at the core of developments in cloud-based technology.

There are many different web-based programming languages; two of them are SQL and PHP. Some of the more notable others include ASP, ASP.NET, Perl, and JSP.

Each web-based programming language has its own advantages and disadvantages.

By storing data in web-based databases, new web technologies have led to 'distributed applications'.

Distributed application programs have many parts that are stored on different virtual machines.

The different virtual machines can be on the same or even different systems, allowing smartphones to access the same resources as desktop computers.

Exam tip

You must be able to use databases from within your own web-based applications.

Web-based vs client–server applications

There used to be two kinds of distributed software:

- **Web-based** software is usually paid for on a subscription or usage basis, allowing companies to pay only for what they need and to grow into the system without large upfront costs.
- **Client–server** software is usually paid for upfront and the initial cost of the system can be high.

Client–server applications have advantages over web-based applications:

- You are in control of upgrades and don't have to update to the latest version if you don't want to.
- You have to manage your systems and pay for technical support.
- Applications tend to run faster when they are local to the user's computer.

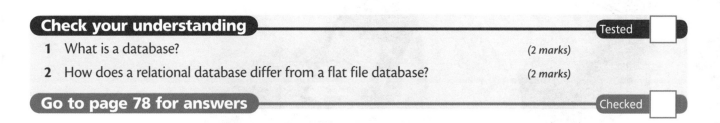

Check your understanding   Tested

1   What is a database?   *(2 marks)*

2   How does a relational database differ from a flat file database? *(2 marks)*

Go to page 78 for answers   Checked

3.1.16 The use of computer technology in society

The use of computer technology in society is growing exponentially.

The use of computing technologies has never been so popular:

- Our lives are fully integrated into a computer science world of **mobile devices**, **tablet computers**, **desktops** and **laptop computers**.

- It is hard to imagine our lives without a connection to the web.

- Originally this connection was only available via wired networks.

- The invention of wireless systems (such as **WiFi (Wireless Fidelity)**, where the connection is through a **router** at home or through wireless hotspots) changed the way we access and use the internet.

↑ **Figure 16.1 Common computing devices**

New uses of technology

Revised

Every day **social media** is changing the way we communicate and interact. It even plays an important motivational role in getting people involved in political and social debates.

Recent research studies have increasingly suggested that the gap between our 'real' world and the 'virtual' world is significantly decreasing.

One of the biggest advances in the use of computers in society has been in the medical industry. Not only have advances in monitoring equipment revolutionised medical treatments but also microprocessors are used in everything from artificial limbs to communication devices using eye movements and blow straws.

The growth of the internet

Most devices are becoming web enabled, which means that they are connected to each other by the internet.

Even software applications are becoming 'cloud based'. This has fundamentally changed the way computer scientists think about computing and programming.

This growth has led to many benefits and drawbacks including **ethical issues** and a growing **digital divide**.

The cloud

↑ **Figure 16.2 Computers connected to each other using the internet**

Ethical issues

Ethical issues involving computers include:

- stealing software – making/using illegal copies
- plagiarising
- making illegal or unethical use of ICT facilities such as accessing inappropriate or offensive websites
- damaging, destroying, stealing, and illegally using ICT facilities and files that belong to others
- cyberbullying
- hacking
- piracy
- waste disposal.

The digital divide

The term 'digital divide' refers to the gap between people with effective access to digital and information communication technology and those with very limited or no access at all.

Many people, mostly those already poor or socially disadvantaged in some other way, cannot or do not have access to the new technologies and the opportunities they bring.

These people – 'socially excluded' in the current jargon – stand on the wrong side of the 'digital divide'.

The digital divide can exist because of a number of reasons:

- **Geographic location**: Some countries lack the infrastructure needs to support ICT.

- **Income**: Some people lack the financial resources to purchase the technology.

    Gender: Some technologies are more attractive to one gender than another.

    Knowledge and skills: Some people lack the knowledge and skills to make use of the technology.

The digital divide includes the imbalances in physical access to technology as well as the imbalances in resources and skills needed to participate effectively as a digital citizen.

Exam tip

You should be able to evaluate the impact of and issues related to the use of computer technology in society,

Intellectual property (IP)   Revised

Intellectual property (IP) refers to creations of the mind: inventions, literary and artistic works, and symbols, names, images, and designs used in commerce.

IP is divided into two categories:

    industrial property, which includes inventions (patents), trademarks, industrial designs, and geographic indications of source

    copyright.

Check your understanding   Tested

1   Why is the copying of software illegal?   *(4 marks)*

2   Explain the digital divide.   *(6 marks)*

Go to page 78 for answers   Checked

3.1.1 Constants, variables and data types

Check your understanding page 11

1 8   5   103   98   −935

2 A real data type contains numeric data in a decimal form. It is used in situations where more accurate information is required than an integer (a whole number) can provide.

3 Storage: Real data takes up more memory than integer data; The number has decimals.

   Processing speed: Calculations using real numbers takes longer than using whole numbers held as integers.

4 If ("door is open") AND ("is cold outside") then "wear coat"

   or

   If door=1 AND cold=1 then coat

5 A string, or text, data type is capable of holding any alphanumeric character (letters, numbers or symbols). It is also capable of storing non-printable characters, such as carriage returns, punctuation characters and spaces. The data within a string data type can consist of a combination of letters, numbers and symbols.

6 Variables are data entities whose values can be altered when a program is compiled. As their name implies, their values vary.

7 The 'print' statement is executed if wet AND cold are both true OR if poor AND hungry are both true.

8 b

3.1.2 Structures

Check your understanding page 13

1 The study of data structures is about organising data so that it is suitable for computer processing.

2 'Concurrent' means happening at the same time as something else.

3 A one-dimensional array is a list of variables. To create an array, you must first define an array variable of the desired type. One-dimensional arrays in Python and PHP allow a list of items to be stored with the capability of accessing each item by pointing to its location within the array, for example:

```
carMakers = ["Ford", "Land Rover",
"Vauxhall", "Nissan", "Toyota"]
```

   or

```
<?php $carMakers = array[Ford, Land Rover,
Vauxhall, Nissan, Toyota]; ?>
```

4 Two-dimensional arrays are nothing more than an array of arrays, in other words an array in one row and another in the next row.

5 It is common practice within programming for the first element within an array to be given an index of zero rather than 1, because 0 is considered by most mathematicians to be a real number between −1 and 1 and so in languages where arrays are positively indexed, zero is the first number (negative indexes are not possible).

6
```php
<?php
$car_name = carMakers[4];
?>
```

3.1.3 Program flow control

Check your understanding page 16

1 The basic building blocks are: sequence, selection and looping.

Sequence example: Set, Input, and Output statements

Selection example: Conditional, if and if–else statements

Looping example: Iteration, While and Do–While statements

2

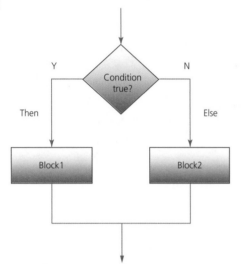

3

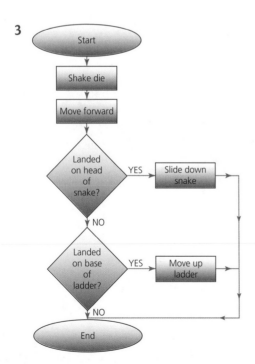

3.1.4 Procedures and functions

1 Procedures and functions allow the repetition of certain sections of a program or calculation many times. They also assist in the modulation of code by allowing themselves to be called from any point within a program solution.

2 A function carries out actions and returns a value to the main program. A procedure carries out actions without returning a value.

3.1.5 Scope of variables, constants, functions and procedures

1 A variable that can be accessed from anywhere within the project that contains its declaration as well as from other projects that refer to that initial project.

2 The scope of a local variable is the procedure in which it is declared. The scope of a global variable is the whole program.

3.1.6 Error handling

1 Syntax errors

Run-time errors

Logic errors

2 The correct name is 'syntax error' and it relates to the grammar rules of the programming language used. These errors are usually due to using the wrong case, placing punctuation in positions where it should not exist or failing to insert punctuation where it should be placed within the code.

3 Called 'run-time errors', these errors occur when the program instructs the computer to carry out an operation that it is either not designed to do or slow to do. It causes a crash or slow running of the code.

4 Logic errors are the most difficult kind of errors to detect and rectify. The program runs successfully but produces incorrect results.

5 Dry-run testing is usually carried out on the algorithm, written in pseudo-code or as part of a flowchart and before the program code is written.

6 A 'trace table' is a technique used to test an algorithm to see if logic errors occur while it is being processed. Each column contains a variable and each row displays the numerical inputs into the algorithm and the resultant values of the variables.

7 b

3.1.7 Handling external data

1 Note: this can be in any programming language. The sample answer is in PHP:

```
<?PHP
 $myFile = "testFile.txt";
 $handle = fopen($myFile, 'w') or die("can't
 open file");
 $stringData = "Steve Cushing\n";
 fwrite($handle, $stringData);
 $stringData = "Ian Cushing\n";
 fwrite($handle, $stringData);
 fclose($handle);
 ?>
```

2 A database is used when you need to store and retrieve large amounts of data. For example, in a web-based membership scheme, your program has to talk to a database.

3 SELECT, UPDATE, DELETE, INSERT

4 a

3.1.8 Computer structure

3.1.8.1 Systems

1 Input, output, process and storage.

2 Any 3 of: a keyboard, a mouse, a scanner, a microphone.

3 Monitor, speakers, printer.

4 Computer systems will break down eventually and so there is a need for strategies to deal with this. With regard to computer systems the method that is used is called 'redundancy'. Redundancy is a method of breakdown prevention where important parts of a system are duplicated so that in the event of a failure the other components can take its place.

3.1.8.3 CPU (Central Processing Unit)

1 This internal device is often referred to as the 'computer's brain' and it is the piece of hardware that is responsible for the 'compute' in computer.

2 'Processor' is a more generic term. There will be other processors in a computing system but only one CPU.

3 a

4 The motherboard is like your nervous system – it provides the essential connections that send and receive signals throughout the system. The bus speed defines how much data the motherboard bus can handle at any one time; the more data, the faster the system.

5 b

3.1.8.4 Memory

Check your understanding page 32

1 Non-volatile memory is memory that retains its information when the power is turned off; volatile memory loses everything if it has no power.

2 Cache memory is the memory closest to the CPU. All the recent instructions are stored in cache memory as it is very fast. A cache memory often has an access time of 100ns, while main memory may have an access time of 700ns. Cache memory is very expensive and hence is limited in capacity.

3 The two types of RAM are DRAM (Dynamic Random Access Memory); SRAM (Static Random Access Memory). RAM is a type of computer memory that can be accessed randomly (any byte of memory can be accessed without touching the preceding bytes); RAM is the most common type of memory found in computers and other devices, such as printers.

4 b

3.1.8.5 Secondary storage

Check your understanding page 33

1 Main memory is sometimes called RAM. It is directly connected to a processor and has fast access times. It also has a smaller capacity than storage devices and costs more per storage unit (i.e. byte).

Secondary storage devices come in many forms including hard drives, USB flash drives, CD/DVD drives and tape drives. These devices are connected to the computer via an internal I/O port and have slower access times than to RAM. In addition, these devices are designed to have much larger capacities for data and the cost per storage unit is very low.

2 Main memory is where your documents exist while you are working on them. When you save, they are stored on a secondary storage device.

3.1.9 Algorithms

1 An algorithm in programming is a step-by-step process that solves a problem in code.

2 An algorithm can be represented by code or by flowcharts.

3

```
Input num[1], num[2], num[3], ..., num[N]
Set Max = num[1]
Set index = 2
While index <= N Do
    If num[index] > Max
        Set Max = num[index]
    Increment index
End While
Output Max
```

4

```
Input num[1], num[2], num[3], ..., num[N]
Set index = 1
While index <= N Do
    Set Sum = Sum + num[index]
    Set Prod = Prod * num[index]
    Increment index
End While
Output Sum and Prod
```

3.1.10 Data representation

1 b

2 High-level languages:
- have more abstractions than lower level languages
- are either compiled or interpreted but low-level languages do not need this type of processing
- are more human readable than low-level languages.

Low-level languages are more efficient than high-level languages.

3 11100000000

To do the conversion, we repeatedly divide by 2:

Operation	Quotient	Remainder	Binary result
1792 ÷ 2 =	896	0	0
896 ÷ 2 =	448	0	00
448 ÷ 2 =	224	0	000
224 ÷ 2 =	112	0	0000
112 ÷ 2 =	56	0	00000
56 ÷ 2 =	28	0	000000
28 ÷ 2 =	14	0	0000000
14 ÷ 2 =	7	0	00000000
7 ÷ 2 =	3	1	100000000
3 ÷ 2 =	1	1	1100000000
1 ÷ 2 =	0	1	11100000000

4 BEEF

To do the conversion, we repeatedly divide by 16:

Operation	Quotient	Remainder	Hexadecimal result
48879 ÷ 16 =	3054	15	F
3054 ÷ 16 =	190	14	EF
190 ÷ 16 =	11	14	EEF
11 ÷ 16 =	0	11	BEEF

3.1.11 Software development life cycle

Check your understanding page 45

1 Requirements, Design, Implementation, Testing, Evolution

2 During the testing phase, the implementation is tested against the specification requirements to ensure that the product is actually providing a solution to the needs addressed and gathered during the requirements phase.

3 Advantages: high degree of risk analysis; excellent model for large and mission-critical projects; software is produced early.

Disadvantages (2 from): can be costly; risk analysis requires highly specific expertise; success is highly dependent on the risk analysis phase.

3.1.11.1 Prototyping

Check your understanding page 47

1 Prototyping offers people who have an interest in a system the capability of evaluating the proposed designs, rather than having to interpret those designs based on some other means such as descriptions.

2 Advantages: the customer and the developer can compare if the developed software matches the software specification; can improve the quality and definition of a customer's requirements; users understand the fundamental issues of the problem better.

Disadvantages: user confusion between prototype and finished system; developer attachment to prototype; excessive development time of the prototype; expense of implementing prototyping.

3.1.12 Application testing

Check your understanding page 50

1 When you write a program, it is very likely that there will be bugs in the program that cause it not to work with certain input data. Therefore, you should test your programs with several input data combinations to ensure as for as possible that the program is correct.

3.1.13 Networking

Check your understanding page 55

1 A computer network connects two or more computers through communication media; it allows the connected computers to exchange information and data and to use the resources of other computers.

2 Clients are computers that use the services of a server. Clients are usually less powerful than the server.

3 c

4 a

5 Advantages (any 5 of):
   - users can share software stored in a main system
   - site (network) licenses for software are less expensive than several standalone licenses
   - files can be shared between users
   - users can communicate via email, instant messenger and VoIP
   - security is of a high standard
   - it is much more straightforward to back up data to a file server
   - data can be transmitted to remote areas

- users can share common peripheral resources such as printers, fax machines, modems etc. therefore saving money.

Disadvantages (any 5 of):

- cabling and file servers can be costly
- management is complicated, requiring training and a specialist network manager
- if a file server breaks down, the files contained on it become inaccessible
- if a virus gets into the system, it can easily spread to other computers
- there is a risk of hacking, particularly with wide area networks
- stringent security measures are required.

3.1.13.1 Client–server

Check your understanding page 57

1 A protocol is a set of rules that governs the transfer of data between computers; it determines the speed of transmission, size of bytes, error checking methods, and whether communication will be asynchronous or synchronous.

Handshaking establishes which protocols to use and controls the flow of data between the computers.

2 A data source (where the data originates); a transmitter (a device used to transmit data from its source); a transmission medium (cables or other data transfer method); a receiver (a device used to receive data); a destination (where the data will be placed or displayed).

3.1.13.2 Web application concepts

Check your understanding page 59

1 Advantages of client–server networks:

- Everything is centralised and managed in one place. Access rights and resource allocation are all done by servers.
- All the files are stored at the same place. In this way, finding files and file management is easy.
- Back up and recovery is much simpler and often automatic.
- Updates, new resources and systems can be added by making necessary changes in the server.
- The server can be accessed remotely across different devices.
- As new information is uploaded to a server database, each workstation does not need to have its own storage capacities increased.
- Server-side security is much more robust.

Disadvantages of client–server networks:

- Too many requests from the clients may lead to congestion.

- If you are downloading a file from a server and it gets abandoned due to some error, the download stops altogether.
- It is very expensive to install and manage this type of computing.
- You need professional IT people to maintain the servers and network.

3.1.14 Use of external code sources

Check your understanding page 61

1 A web mashup is a web page or coded application used to combine data or functionality from two or more sources to create a new product.

2 An IFrame (Inline Frame) is an HTML document embedded inside another HTML document; it is used to embed content from another source into a Web page.

3 API stands for Application Programming Interface; an interface is a common boundary between two systems; an API allows code on two different systems to communicate with each other.

3.1.15 Database concepts

Check your understanding page 65

1 Databases use a series of tables to store the data. A table is a two-dimensional representation of data stored in rows and columns.

2 A flat file database has one table, similar to a spreadsheet. A relational database has multiple linked tables.

3.1.16 The use of computer technology in society

Check your understanding page 68

1 Companies spend a large amount of money designing, developing and marketing software. If people copy it, they steal the intellectual property rights and stop the company from making money. This can prevent new games and software being developed.

2 The digital divide is the gap between people who can access technology and people who cannot. This could be a simple as a person being able to buy things cheaper online than someone without the technology but can also refer to countries that have no easy access to the internet and all it offers in terms of education and knowledge.